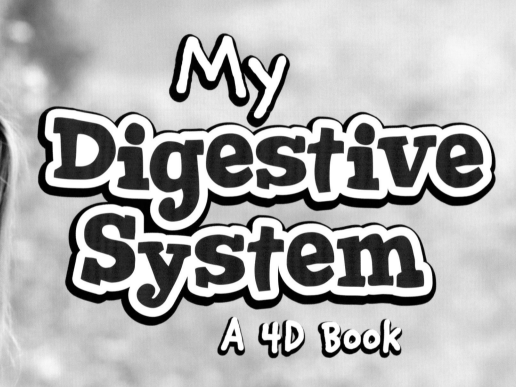

My Digestive System

A 4D Book

by Emily Raij

Consultant:
Natasha Kasbekar, M.D., Pediatrician
Kids Health Partners, LLC, Skokie, Ill.

PEBBLE
a capstone imprint

Pebble Plus is published by Pebble
1710 Roe Crest Drive, North Mankato, Minnesota 56003
www.mycapstone.com

Library of Congress Cataloging-in-Publication Data
Library of Congress Cataloging-in-Publication data is available
on the Library of Congress website.
ISBN 978-1-9771-0234-8 (library binding)
ISBN 978-1-9771-0550-9 (paperback)
ISBN 978-1-9771-0236-2 (eBook PDF)
Provides facts about the digestive system.

Editorial Credits
Karen Aleo and Anna Butzer, editors; Charmaine Whitman, designer;
Kelly Garvin, media researcher; Katy LaVigne, production specialist

Image Credits
iStockphoto: Steve Debenport, 7, Ulianna, 5; Shutterstock: arborelza, 17,
eveleen, 11, GraphicsRF, 15, ilusmedical, cover (inset), Juta, 1, kareinoppe,
9, Lightspring, 13, LooksLikeLisa, 19, Monkey Business Images, cover, 21,
Tetiana Saienko, cover (inset)
Artistic elements: Shutterstock/dmitriyio

Printed and bound in China.
970

Note to Parents and Teachers

The My Body Systems set supports the national science
standards related to structures and processes. This book
describes and illustrates the digestive system. The images
support early readers in understanding the text. The
repetition of words and phrases helps early readers learn
new words. This book also introduces early readers to
subject-specific vocabulary words, which are defined in
the Glossary section. Early readers may need assistance
to read some words and to use the Table of Contents,
Glossary, Read More, Internet Sites, Critical Thinking
Questions, and Index sections of the book.

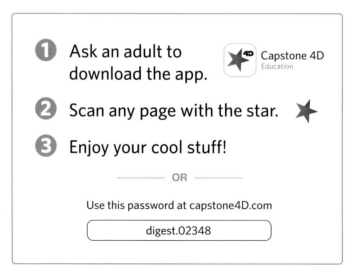

1 Ask an adult to download the app.

Capstone 4D
Education

2 Scan any page with the star.

3 Enjoy your cool stuff!

— OR —

Use this password at capstone4D.com

digest.02348

Table of Contents

Food Goes In 4

Following Food 8

Keeping Healthy 18

Glossary 22

Read More 23

Internet Sites 23

Critical Thinking Questions 24

Index 24

Food Goes In

Yum! I smell pizza.

My mouth starts to water.

Now my stomach rumbles.

Before I take a bite, my

digestive system starts working!

Food gives my body nutrients.

My body helps break down food.

It turns the food I eat into energy.

Then I can play and grow.

Following Food

My teeth bite food and

mash it into smaller pieces.

Saliva forms in my mouth.

This spit makes the food

softer and easier to swallow.

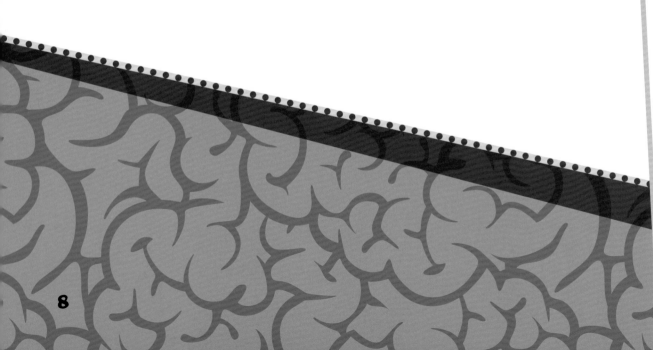

My tongue moves the soft food
into a ball. Now it's ready
to swallow. It goes down
my throat into a tube
called the esophagus.

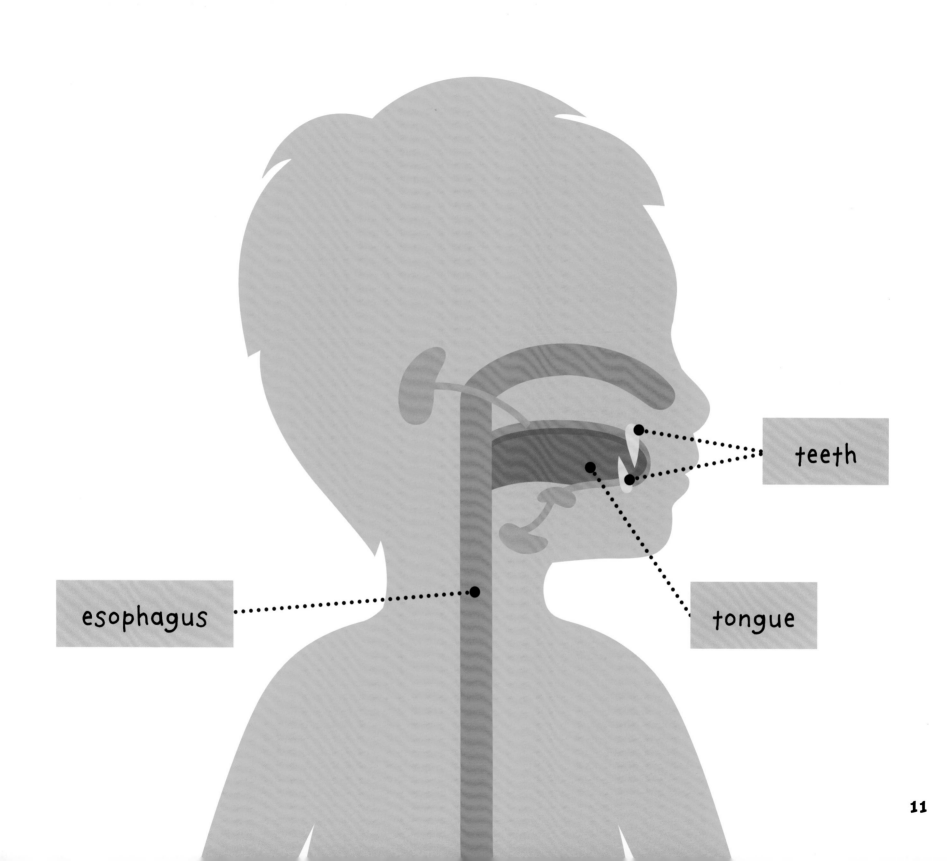

teeth

esophagus

tongue

Esophagus muscles move food
into my stretchy stomach.
Digestive juices break down
food into smaller pieces.

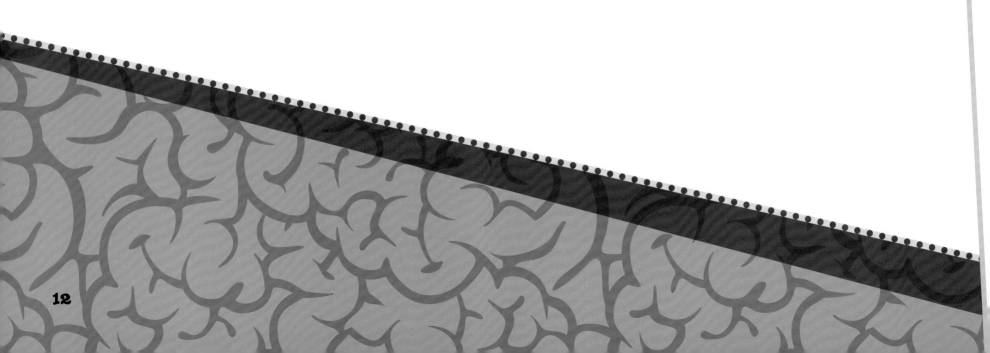

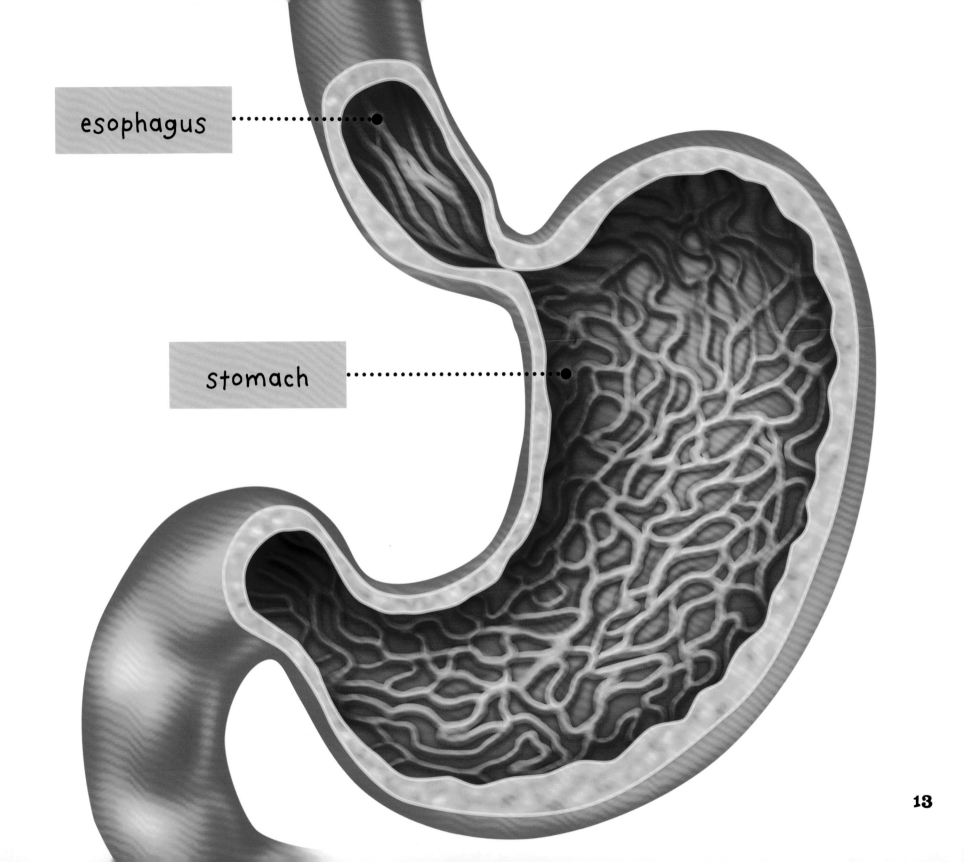

esophagus

stomach

13

The food mix moves into
my small intestine. Nutrients
pass into my blood here.
Next my large intestine
collects water and waste.

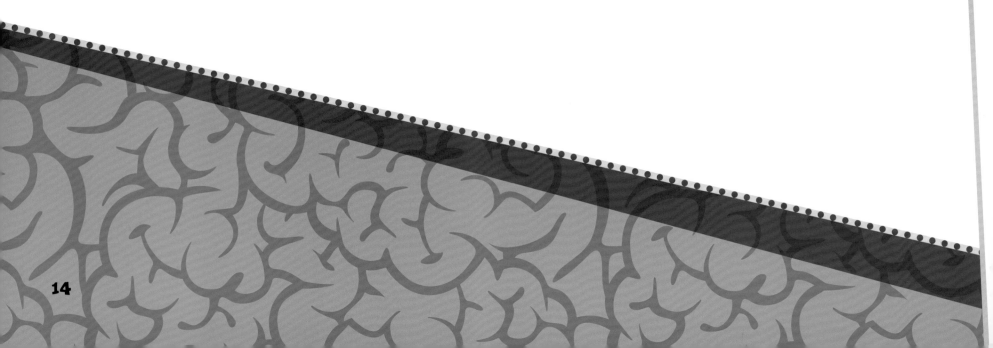

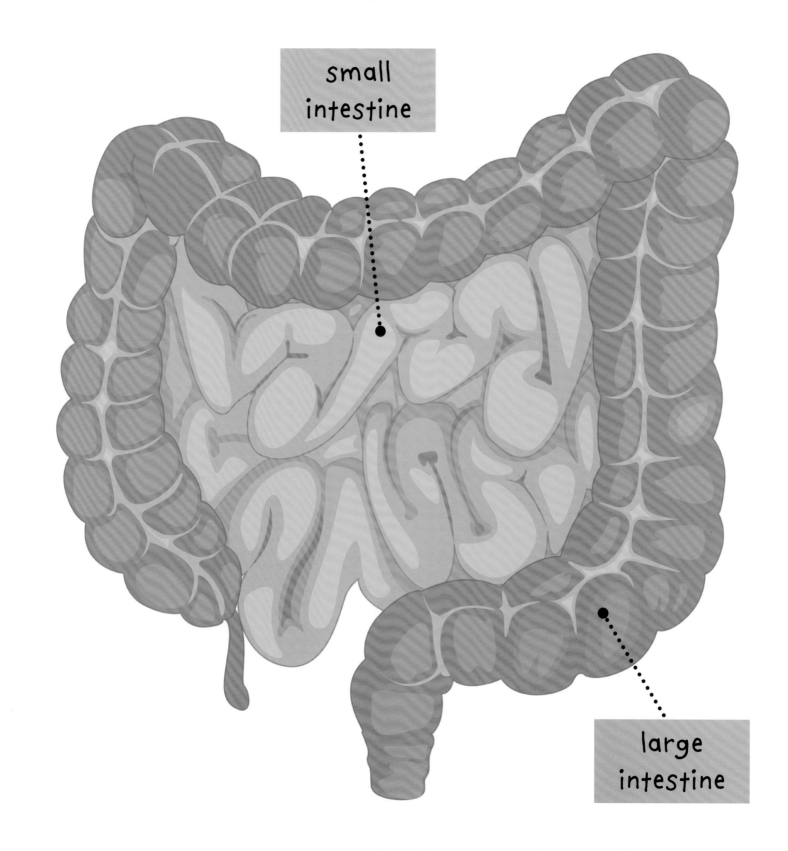

small
intestine

large
intestine

Water is sent to my blood.

Waste is pushed into my rectum.

It stays here until I am

ready to use the bathroom.

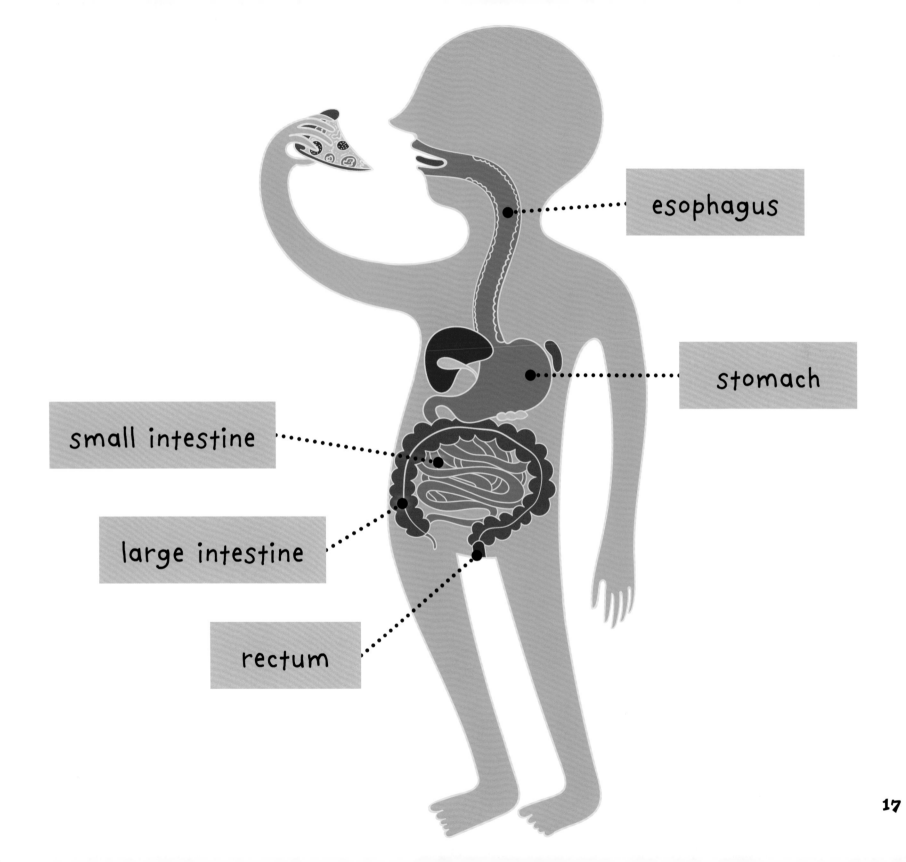

esophagus

stomach

small intestine

large intestine

rectum

Keeping Healthy

I use my hands to eat.

I need to wash my food

and hands so germs

don't make me sick.

19

I make sure to eat right.

Healthy food is good for me.

It gives me energy.

I help my digestive system

so it helps me.

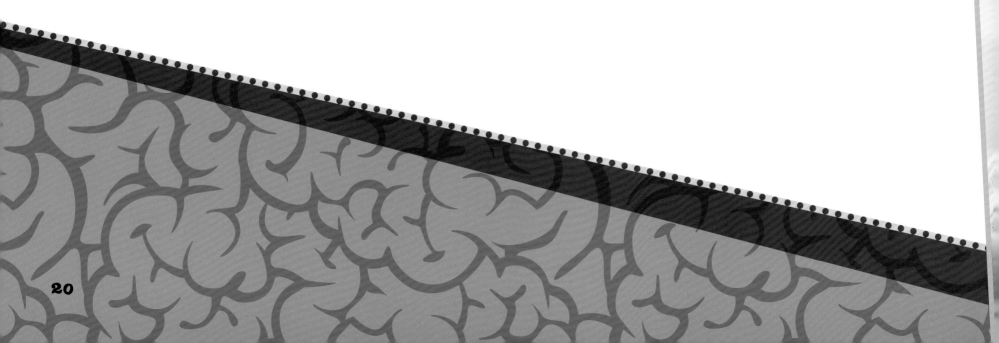

21

Glossary

energy—the strength to do active things without getting tired

esophagus—a long tube from the mouth to the stomach

germ—a tiny living thing that causes sickness

large intestine—a tube that is the last part of the digestive system; the large intestine pushes solid waste matter out of the body

muscle—a tissue in the body that is made of strong fibers

nutrient—something that is needed by people, animals, and plants to stay healthy and strong

rectum—the final, straight part of the large intestine

saliva—the clear liquid in the mouth

small intestine—a long tube between the stomach and the large intestine

waste—food that the body gets rid of after it has been digested

Read More

Brett, Flora. *Your Digestive System Works!* Your Body Systems. North Mankato, Minn.: Capstone Press, 2015.

Kolpin, Molly. *Why Do I Burp?* My Silly Body. North Mankato, Minn.: Capstone Press, 2015.

Pimentel, Annette Bay. *My Stomach.* Inside My Body. Mankato, Minn.: Amicus Illustrated, 2016.

Internet Sites

Use FactHound to find Internet sites related to this book.

Visit *www.facthound.com*

Just type in 9781977102348 and go.

Super-cool stuff!

Check out projects, games and lots more at
www.capstonekids.com

Critical Thinking Questions

1. What do your small and large intestines do?

2. How does your body get rid of waste?

3. How can you keep your digestive system healthy?

Index

blood, 14, 16

energy, 6, 20

food, 4, 6, 8, 10, 12, 14, 18, 20

germs, 18

intestines, 14

mouth, 4, 8

muscles, 12

nutrients, 6, 14

rectum, 16

saliva, 8

stomach, 4, 12

throat, 10